The View in Winter

A Book of Poems
by Margery Wells Steer

Watercolors
by Alice Steer Wilson

Enjoy!
Janica Wilson
Birdick

southbound press

Winter Morning First Snow
1991

He stands inside the window, looking out
Both little hands pressed flat upon the pane

What happened to his world last night?
He views it all with wonder and delight

Great Grandma shares the view
Seen by this child of two
The snows of more than ninety years have fallen
Where is the world she knew
When she was only two?
And still the snow at night
Brings wonder and delight
She cannot understand the world she sees
But she has made her peace with mysteries

Foreword

When I asked my daughter, Alice Steer Wilson, to do the illustrations for "The View In Winter" she was delighted. Although she has always been my first reader, she welcomed this new way to collaborate.

For many years my friend Margaret Apgar and I have shared our interest in the written word, and I am grateful for her hours of typing and editorial help. My first grandchild, Janice Wilson Stridick, has provided fresh vision for my work by serving as publisher and final editor of this volume.

I have tried several times to write an adequate paragraph of thanks to my helpers who have made possible this sharing of my view in winter. Each time I failed and tore it up. So I will just say that my debt to them is enormous and my thanks comes from my heart.

Winter . . . that quiet time of deep snows and warm fires . . . dreaming of things past and things to come. A time of waiting for another spring.

So here it is – my view in the winter of my ninety-second year.

Margery Wells Steer

Margery Wells Steer
Friends House, Sandy Spring, Maryland
Fall of 1991

Table of Contents

Song of a Skywatcher

July 1991

I am a loiterer
I take my time
I do not hurry . . . linger on the way
To notice what the roadside offers me

I am a collector
Of trivia and trifles
Old letters, clippings, pictures
And curious little artifacts
That have no meaning
To anyone but me

I am an explorer
Of little roads to nowhere
I want to find surprises they may hold
I get entangled in the underbrush
Of small irreverent thoughts
And stories to be told

I delight in delay
I look around, enjoying the view
And seeking some new thought
To bring to you

But you are like a bird
That makes incredible journeys through the sky
You touch the earth
And then, refreshed, press on
To keep your strange appointment
With a special time and place
And I must reconsider
Much I thought I knew
About such things as minutes on a clock
And miles to go

What joy to watch you
In your swift, sure flight
With some mysterious guidance
Day and night
Be patient with this watcher of the sky
You wonder at its mysteries
And so do I

Spring Water

To write a book . . . compose a song
I have left these things too long
What have I to give you then
As an offering from my pen?
Columns . . . letters . . . lots of chaff
And once in a while a hearty laugh

Like water in the hidden springs
My thoughts run deep on many things
If now and then a truth profound
Finds its way up from underground
Bring me a little paper cup
Together we will drink it up

13   *Marge on Marge*

Garden People

All day they stand there looking slightly stupid
They do not toil and neither do they spin
They do not plow or plant or harvest
They simply keep the geese from coming in

These people are of man's – not God's – creation
Composed of sticks and shabby, worn-out clothes
Their makers did the best they could, but still
It's hard to take much pride in one of those

God made the goose a thing of flying beauty
A scarecrow merely stands and does his duty

Food for Thought

When the human race was very young
The dinner bell was never rung
When hungry, folks just looked around
And were content with what they found

Just like mankind, I was a child
Who found that food was growing wild
In the sandy bottom of our bay
Hard-shell clams lived hid away
And oftentimes my searching toes
Would discover some of those
Along the shore the beach plums sweet
Provided us another treat
Wild cherry joy was not complete
They left red stains on our bare feet
Roadside berries, black and red,
Were other things on which we fed

In autumn woods, with colors bright,
It was our very great delight
In fallen leaves, down on our knees
To look for nuts from chestnut trees
How great our joy and our surprise
When food came falling from the skies!

Dinner Order

My hair is gray, my eyes are blue
And I am Yankee through and through
For Boston beans I greatly wish
Clam chowder is a favorite dish
I always think I am in luck
When I can eat Long Island duck

If in the Midwest you were born
Of course you're very fond of corn
And baked potatoes you should know
Grow very well in Idaho
And if you thrill to none of these
Perhaps you like Wisconsin cheese
With these delicious things to eat
Excuse me, please, from Shredded Wheat
An awful way
To start the day
With something that tastes just like hay!

A Special Correspondent

I do not think that spelling ought
To hinder the free flow of thought
I have a friend who writes to me
Who never won a spelling bee
She never ever thinks to look
In Mr. Webster's monstrous book
To use a word like rhapsodizes
She plunges in and improvises
Her spelling used to make me wince
But I got over that long since

Her letters never fail to please
For they are like a fresh spring breeze
Which through the windows of my room
Bring visions of the flowers in bloom
Her spelling tests she could not pass
But she is in that special class
Of those who make my life much better
By the magic of the personal letter

To Janice Griffin

From Generation to Generation

My grandfather Binkerd could hardly bear
The way I chose to wear my hair
Said he, "When I look at you it appears
You have no forehead . . . you have no ears"

Today it's a somewhat similar story
I look at my granddaughters' crowning glory
And think that improvement could be made
With the help of some hairpins and comb or a braid

From the appearance of their heads
I judge they recently rose from their beds
Or were caught out-of-doors with a strong wind blowing
Have they looked in the mirror? There's no way of knowing

But this I have learned as I have grown older
Beauty's in the eye of the youthful beholder
What an amazement! What a surprise!
When I look at the world through
my granddaughters' eyes!

Hair styles will vary in times and in places
But nothing can alter their beautiful faces
I should remember what I have forgot
They may wish I'd get rid of my old granny knot

One Red Leaf

The wind has left me one red leaf
One blazing scarlet leaf
Plastered against my window pane

It is enough
To tell me fall has kept its date
With humankind
And left this lovely calling card behind

24 Congress Street

Cape May, New Jersey

Our daughter's house is sheltered by a tree
That's old and crooked and a lot like me
It has seen many more productive days
Some think that it should go and yet it stays
To cast its present thin and scanty shade
Where once Victorian parents sat and children played

Nostalgia

In Memoriam

I'll come again but I'll no longer see
That old and twisted paper mulberry tree
Much loved, it had lived out its many days
Its owner and the watching neighbors gazed
As it came down. It soon was carried away
And on our calendar we marked this special day

The wrenching winter winds and all the snow
The flowing sap of spring which made it grow
The withering heat of summer and the salty breeze
It had enjoyed and suffered all of these
It had survived the anxious care of man
That never was a part of Nature's plan
It had endured the batterings of life
But it could not escape the final knife
Next year I'll see a new tree in its place
A strong, young tree . . . But it will not erase
The memory of that fine old mulberry tree
Which sheltered that old house so near the sea

Scene at the Seashore

In bygone Mid-Victorian days
Proper ladies all wore stays
Strolling on the beach dressed neatly
They were covered up completely
Tall or short or fat or thin
They were clothed from toe to chin

Gossip in a Graveyard

Here lie my Northville neighbors
Long may they rest in peace
From all their human joys and woes
Enjoying sweet release
I'm sure it would surprise them
To know it was their fate
That I would be remembering them
In nineteen eighty-eight!

Here lies a man who lived for years alone
He now lies still beneath this mossy stone
In independence he took greatest pride
Was it of utter boredom that he died?

And here she lies, a jolly cheerful soul
To help her neighbors was her chosen role
No better pies than hers were ever made
She was a pillar of the Ladies Aid
Until at last she took her final breath
Some say that laughing caused her death

Two youths went forth with guns to hunt wild game
(Both of them bore the same ancestral name)
There was an accidental, fatal shot
And one of them came home . . . and one did not
One died. One lived for years, and yet
I doubt that he was able to forget
The shot that day that echoed all around
The woods that bordered our Long Island Sound
They both lie here on this day in September
Am I the only one left to remember?

Old Ed's voice made a booming sound
Heard by his neighbors all around
He lost his voice when he fell ill
And all the town grew very still
When he arrived at Heaven's gate
Impatient of the slightest wait
Did he give forth a mighty shout
To let God know he was without?

Here lies a member of our choir
To be like her was my desire
Her hair was golden . . . mine was not
I fell in love right on the spot
And also very unlike me
She never ever sang off key
To all she was a special friend
Did she go singing to the end?

I look for a stone I do not find
Which calls a tragic tale to mind
Once on a chilly autumn night
When the moon was shining bright
She walked out in Long Island Sound
And then forgot to turn around
She walked where the water was very deep
Some say she was walking in her sleep
But others knew that her life was sad
She longed for things she never had
They looked for her along the shore
But knew Aunt Lillie was no more

Once long ago we drove a horse
And never heard the word divorce
And then a teacher came to town
(As I recall, her name was Brown)
She boarded with a childless pair
And soon the rumors filled the air
Divorce, that awful, shocking act,
In time became a legal fact
The news that day quite stunned the town
Her name henceforth was not Miss Brown
Talk in the town went round and round
And now all three lie underground

I think perhaps it's just as well
There are some things that stones don't tell

If Stones Could Speak
1991

Shorelines . . . a part of the creation
That have for me a fascination
They hold in check the mighty sea
Two miles of them belong to me
In every inlet, sound and bay
Through all the centuries they say
In tones not very loud but clear
"Come no farther; stop right here."
But the sea resists the circling shores
With gentle bites and fearsome roars

II

Pebbles like gems along the water's edge
Washed by the tides;
The sedge grass and the beach pea's blooming vine;
Bayberry bushes with the leaves
That, crushed in children's hands,
Gave forth their fragrance;
The bordering woods with their storm-battered trees
Festooned with the wild grape
And catbriers lurking in the underbrush;
And when night came, there was the sky
The setting sun
And driftwood fires
And far off in the distance there was the gleam

Of Horton's Light
These all were mine
My heritage from many generations past
This was the background of my early years

III

The contours of my shore
With time have changed
The wilderness is gone
So is the pier that in times past
Served passing ships with cargo to unload
For ancestors of mine
Living in simple homes upon their farms
The summer people now are everywhere
I do not know their names

IV

But I am told two landmarks still remain
Two rocks stand steadfast in their places
Some mighty force in geologic time
Has left them there
Immovable by man

V

The Penny Rock stands on the beach
Of the Penny family farm
Beyond the reach of the tides
As seasons pass, barren and bare it stands
No living thing can find a foothold there
Sometimes adventurous children
Try to scale its sides to reach its top
Then tire of it and pass it by

VI

But Half-Mile Rock
Is quite another thing
From on my shore we only see
A little part of it
Some more – some less –
According to the tide

Old men may speculate at length
About its size
Extending down into the deeps no man can see
The mussels and the barnacles
Find it a place to grow
And who knows what other forms of life
Make it a home far down below

The Penny Rock had nothing to conceal
And any casual stroller on the beach
Could see its monstrous size
Its warm brown tones

But Half-Mile Rock was far off shore
Too far to venture often in our flimsy boat
But I remember that there was a day
When we went all the way
And saw the wet growth close up at the waterline
Imagined all the teeming world of life below
But still the rock its dangerous secrets kept

So we rowed home
To our familiar shore
Still wondering –
And no wiser
Than we were before

VII

If rocks could speak
What would these two rocks say?
Will even they
Know change and disappear
Some future day?

Winterview

Over the brow of the hill of history
Come the shining troops

Our beloved children
Generation after generation of them
Down into the dark valley of war and death
We send them
Generation after generation of them

For what purpose?
To defend an imaginary line, a border, a word –
An idea in the mind of some leader . . .
. . . we call this freedom

Oh bloody century of human sacrifice!
Five times in my lifetime I have seen it happen

Oh weep for all the lost children
Weep!
Toll *all* the bells!

The Weight of a Snowflake

One woman's voice – in one small newspaper
Addressing her neighbors
   in the fields and cowbarns of Ohio
For twenty-three years . . . once each week
850 columns, give or take a few

As for her message? Peace – never changing

Women around the world, *cry out*
The mighty din may shake the walls of every
   mighty power
And then some day
The walls come tumbling down . . . the maps remade

What is the weight of a snowflake?
The weight of many snowflakes?

Winona Meeting House

Serene . . . secure . . . within their meeting house
Beneath the sheltering tree
The little band of silent Quakers wait
No sermon and no soaring hymns of praise
For they are listening
For the voice of God within

No stained glass windows here obstruct the view
Through clear glass windowpanes
They see the gently sloping burying grounds
Where lie the weighty Quakers of the past
And those more lately laid to rest
It is a quiet, truly peaceful scene
And over all the healing grass grows green

One Summer Night

One summer night that I shall not forget
I went with Father to inspect the net
To see if any fish were in it yet

There was no sound except the splash of oars
No light save stars; and on our darkened shores
The landmarks all had vanished from my sight
Far down the beach the gleam of Horton's Light
Guided the vessels passing in the night

Above me is the sky and outer space
Beneath, the sea, that dark mysterious place
And in between, a little child afloat
In one small, fragile, man-made wooden boat

The old, familiar net I scarcely know
Transformed by magic phosphorescent glow
I am surrounded by infinity
A world of beauty and of mystery

The boat is beached
And I must go to bed
A new night world too large within my head
How was a little girl to go to sleep
When she was part of mysteries so deep?

Evensong

I still can read the numbers of each hymn
But words and music now are very dim
But even folks who have defective eyes
Delight to find they still can harmonize
And so from memory I hum along
Adding an alto to the evensong

Some words inscribed upon these hymnbook pages
Come down to us from now forgotten ages
Some thoughts of God herein I find atrocious
Some make the Christians sound a bit ferocious
Speaking of battles, enemies and fights
I like the songs of peace and quiet nights

And as I sing, I see the well-loved faces
Of those who sang in other times and places
I hear their voices as in other days
Joining together in a song of praise

*To Natalie Krakau
and the Sunday evening hymn sings
at Friends' House*

In a Florist's Shop

Your greenhouse flowers on their way
Will speak of love on Mother's Day

I wonder if you understand
That buttercups in a little hot hand
Are more than adequate to convey
Her love for mother on her day

When she gets older, she will buy
Your lovely flowers, and so will I
But this I know; I'd hate to have missed
Those limp bouquets in a small child's fist

Sunny Slope Farm Revisited

April 2, 1988

We knew we would not find the house the same
New owners lost it one dark day in flame
The one they built seems strange and unreal too
It's not the sturdy farmhouse that we knew

Where was the weeping willow in whose shade
The children of the family often played
I seek the garden where our child was wed
And find the ghosts of flowers long since dead
Who now the ample kitchen garden tends?
Its shared abundance gladdened many friends

The fields looked drab. Would there be hay and grain
As once there was when summer comes again?
The barn seemed empty and a bit forlorn
And all about seemed tired and slightly worn

When May comes, will all the orchards bloom
Or have years of neglect now spelled their doom?
Who will redeem the fallen apple loss
By making all those bowls of applesauce?

We did not look but hoped that there was still
An ancient tulip growing on the hill
In all our woods, no other tree so tall
And all its leaves turned yellow in the fall
For us Time wrote with firm, relentless finger
The message "Finished" . . . so we did not linger
But memory brought all back in clear perfection
The farm, that April day, knew resurrection

The Door at Atwood Lake

The wind is sharp; tree branches toss and moan
And all the world outside seems cold as stone
We put more logs upon the dying fire
And see reluctant flames rise ever higher
The noisy waves come crashing on our shore
But all is well within our tight-closed door
A perfect setting for old age in truth
But still we feel some lack . . . that lack is Youth
Two generations of our children came and went
And when these happy interludes were spent
We found we had for our monotonous diet
Too much of what we longed for . . . peace and quiet!

The letter that the postman brought today
Was from a youth whose home was far away
He needs a place for several summer weeks
While he a better understanding seeks
Of ways American, to him so strange
Could we by chance, a home for him arrange?

And so we opened up our safe-closed door
To people we had never known before
And through that door came young folks, one by one,
Five from the land that boasts the Rising Sun
They came from Egypt, France and also Greece
Each brought to us their messages of peace

And there came a charming, dark-eyed boy
Who brought with him no messages of joy
Who recently escaped by just a breath
From scenes of revolution and of death
His family, followers of the Moslem God,
Had narrowly escaped a firing squad
In Bangladesh no horrors he'll now see
He's now a member of our family

Through our small door they all depart at last
To travel on and to rejoin their past
Forever altered by this one brief stay
As we were too because they came our way

A Bar of Soap

She took her neighbors' cans of kitchen grease
And changed them into messages of peace
And far away her bars of homemade soap
Would often speak of cleanliness and hope

And to the needy world she gave a son
Who, through his lifetime labors, was the one
Who found new ways to help the sun and rain
Bring forth the crops to ease the world's deep pain
And thus, through him, some multitudes were fed
Who otherwise would not have daily bread

Today, at ninety-seven, she's gone to rest
And all the village friends who knew her best
Remembering her, won't be content to grumble
But find some way to help, however humble
And I'll recall a life whose widened scope
Carried the symbol of a cake of soap

*Dedicated to Erma Wilson
mother of Fred Wilson
July 1, 1890 - April 20, 1988*

To Margaret in Memory of Larry
April 12, 1989

The hot, bright light of many noons
The silvery, other-worldly light of many moons
From outer space come down their steadfast rays
That mark the rhythm of our passing days

Until the sun goes down we never know
The lingering beauty of the afterglow
It was a year ago that his sun set
Leaving us beauty we cannot forget

His struggles and achievements, joys and pain
We know we shall not ever see again
Still there are melodies I often hear
That to this day will always bring him near

The evening comes and there to our surprise
Are floods of color in the western skies
I think of him and wish that he might know
That I am thankful for his afterglow

MARGE AND JIM
Wedding Day

No guest-filled church
No wedding music on an organ played
No flowers delivered by a florist's truck
That day saw none of these
But solemn promises were made
Beneath the trees

I see it still . . . the home where I grew up
The farmhouse with its cool encircling shade
The lovely linden tree
And all the ancient maples
And the buckeye tree
Beyond the barn, the green potato fields
That seemed to have no end
Were in full bloom
My parents' pride and joy

And all the orange blossoms in the world
Could not compare
With the hope and promise
They saw blooming there

In Lighter Vein

1991

The wedding day of Jim and Marge
Was dawning bright and fair
A garden wedding it would be
With lots of people there

The wedding hour was set for noon
The dew was on the grass
When to our horror someone found
That it had come to pass
That an old farm horse, now retired,
At last gave up the fight
And wandered from the barn to die
In the middle of the night

The death bed scene
In three short hours
Must be transformed
With garden flowers

The family troops were all called out
The corpse was dragged away
And all was carried out as planned
On our wedding day

This family tale
They oft rehearse
Complete . . . each chapter
And each verse

It's funnier now than on that day
They had to haul Old Jep away

Thoughts on an Anniversary
May 14, 1990

Wrapped in myself
And chilly to the bone
The universe around me
Cold as stone

Then I reach out
To touch a human hand
Perhaps of someone
In a distant land

There is an answering touch
I'm not alone
I hear the echo of a voice
I once have known.

There is a reassurance
That we both desire
And so we warm ourselves
By Friendship's fire

Is there some distant land to which you went
When all your years on earth with me were spent?
Is it a land to which I too shall go?
I tell you truly that I do not know

I tell you also that I do not care
To search for answers to the how and where
In farms . . . in gardens . . . in a classroom chair
When I reach out I always find you there

45   *Marge and Jim*

Holy Communion
1991

The forms and symbols
Of the little church
Beneath whose sheltering shadow I grew up
Were strange to him
In Quaker meeting he had never known
Communion Day
The holy hush as bread and wine were passed
And then consumed together
And the gentle click
As empty glasses were replaced
The ritual complete

All this was strange to him
But this no barrier made
Between us. So we were wed

And in due time I learned
That he had forms and rituals of his own
Observed with loving care
He worshipped at the shrines that none could see
And shared his reverence for the land with me

Before the first faint hint of spring was felt
His land must be made ready
The planting of the seed for him a rite
Performed with utmost care

And when the sprouting seed
Broke through the soil
This most miraculous event
Was cause for joy
And family celebration

He suffered with his crops
When scorching sun
Beat down relentlessly
Revived with them when cooling rains
Washed over them

At last came fall
The climax of his year
When he was able
To gather us around the dinner table
There to consume his sacramental meal
The apples, corn and bread
In reverent wonder at the sun and rain and soil
And human care
By which mankind is fed

Be My Guest

October 1990

One by one
My doors out to the world
Slam shut
Homebound
Inside my window I look out
The world is gray
My view grows dim with every passing day
Must I now join the ranks
Of all the lame . . . the halt . . . even the blind?

Resigned
I now retreat into neglected portions
Of my mind
And then invite my friends to join me there
And suddenly I see beyond a doubt
My vision grows more clear
The sun comes out

Clinging Vine

We always wanted to be self-reliant
The weakness of old age makes us defiant
The strong, free-standing people we admired
To be like them we always had aspired
But that's a goal the years make us resign
And now we change our role to clinging vine
Reluctantly we find it is our duty
To show the world another kind of beauty

Bedtime in a Hospital

For all of four days
I have heard no news

Has the world ceased to exist
Because I have not been watching
The floods, the wars, the starving children
And the general woe?

Perhaps it is I who have ceased to exist
To feel compassion, hunger and the need to help

Sunk deep in my small pain
I felt no need to know
How fared the planet and my fellow man

Night falls
Bedtime routines I know
The pills to take
Adjust the blanket
Turn out the light
I shall be home again within the world
Tomorrow night

Reunion

1991

I knew it was no Steinway Concert Grand
It never did pretend to be
What it was not
But from the day it came through our small door
I knew it was – and always would be – mine

Its shiny newness now is worn away
By children's fingers . . . and my own
And by the battering of the passing years
And now we are united once again
For two brief days

It has had several homes
As family needs have changed
One key gives forth no sound
One string no longer vibrates to my touch
But memory fills in the missing note
The melody goes on

The old songs come unbidden . . . play themselves
Through fingers numb and stiffened by old age
I hear the resonance of the cello played
By younger fingers close beside me
I catch the echo of the harmonies we made

And through it all I hear
The obligato of my falling tears
And my light-hearted laughter through the years

Epitaph

She wanted to be a World Improver
In her own small way a Shaker and Mover
To make some bad condition better
She would sit down and write a letter
She couldn't care less about lavish living
Viewed city life with some misgiving
Was committed to the open spaces
Like farms and other country places
To reading and writing she was addicted
And with failing vision was afflicted
Thought competitive games were for the birds
She got her fun from rhyming words
She loved making a home for their children and others
There the young from abroad became sisters and brothers
She was so pro-peace and so anti-war
That she may have become a colossal bore
But the wars went right on till the day of her dying
She didn't succeed but she didn't stop trying
Her thoughts were never very profound
Her feet were firmly on the ground
But she often looked up at the starry sky
And asked the perennial question, "Why?"

This epitaph will find no room
   on any future family tomb
Her ashes to the wind they'll scatter
But that she knows won't greatly matter
Some long forgotten word or deed
Will lodge somewhere, like drifting seed
In some far place find growing room
And in some distant meadow bloom

To the Grandchildren

I once could hear each whisper in the room
And find a shy white violet in bloom
And walk with steady, energetic stride
Down woodland paths and over meadows wide
The senses fail, I miss my former powers
But still I find I have no empty hours
They're filled with all the well-remembered joys
And voices of a host of girls and boys
Who hold the future in uncertain hands
And bind me to the world with steel-strong bands

About the author

Margery Wells Steer was born in New Canaan, Connecticut on August 29, 1899. From the Long Island potato farm where she grew up, to the dairy farm in North Lima, Ohio where she raised her children, to the home on Atwood Lake, Ohio and finally her beloved Friends House in Sandy Spring, Maryland, she has sown seeds of peace and understanding. She was educated at Northfield Seminary (now the Northfield Mt. Herman School) in Northfield, Massachusetts and Oberlin College, Oberlin, Ohio. At Oberlin College, and through her lifelong partnership with her husband James Wilson Steer, she grew to identify with the cause of peace and the work of the Society of Friends. The Quaker community of Winona, Ohio where Jim Steer grew up, was instrumental in her early decisions about peace and international relations.

Her column, "Peace and the People" was carried by the Salem, Ohio "Farm and Dairy" from 1965 until 1988 and she was recognized by the Smith College Women's History Archive for her contribution to journalism. Her views have been published in "Soviet Woman" (long before Perestroika), "The Churchman," "American Heritage," and many others. She and her husband served as 'grandparents' and hosts to many international visitors studying in the United States. She has originated newsletters in several communities in addition to participating in the Friends House writing group, and she has shared many, many poems and stories with family and friends throughout her long life.

About the artist

Alice Steer Wilson, daughter of Margery Wells Steer and James Wilson Steer, was born in Salem, Ohio on November 8, 1926. Like both of her parents, she graduated from Oberlin College. She also studied at Black Mountain College in North Carolina, and the Pennsylvania Academy of the Fine Arts in Philadelphia. She has received numerous awards for her work, and her paintings are included in collections from the United States to Europe and Japan.

About the book

"The View in Winter" was conceived by the author and her daughter. Through the collaboration of Janice Wilson Stridick, granddaughter of the author and daughter of the artist, it has taken form. She pulled the parts together, edited and reworked them, and produced the final layout with the able assistance of designer T. A. Hahn.

On Turning 40
When Grandma's 92

January 1992

My conversation with age began last month

Her poems reach over a century
Her ailments reach into each moment
Sight gone, stomach weak
As we work on her book we're wrapped in her lifetime
A lifeline of good common sense

She never knew luxury
And she wanted for little
She always looked beyond her door
To the places where peace could walk

Margery, my steering star guiding light versifying Grandma!
You read to me at three,
Guided me into the world of words . . .
Walked me into a global field of dreams as a teen . . .
Weaned me from my fancy lingerings as an adult

I drink in your life when all is dry or tainted around me
Knowing that, though imperfect and human,
You stayed a course
I would be honored to keep

jws